Tap a Pan

Written by Rachael Davis

Collins

tap tap

a pan

sit sit

tap tap

5

tap it

tip tip

8

tap it

9

tap tap

pan

pan

pan

tap a pan

13

14

 Review: After reading

Use your assessment from hearing the children read to choose any GPCs and words that need additional practice.

Read 1: Decoding

- Read pages 2 and 6 and check the children's understanding of **tap**. After each page ask: What is the person using to tap? (*a hammer*, *sticks*) Ask the children to mime the actions.
- Point to the word **pan** on page 3. Ask the children to sound out the letters in the word, then blend. (*/p/a/n* – **pan**) Repeat for the words on page 12. If the children cannot work out what the word is, say the sounds, and then say the word. Tell the children to repeat after you.
- Look at the "I spy sounds" pages (14–15). Point to the table, and say "table", emphasising the /t/ sound. Ask the children to find other items in the picture that start with the /t/ sound. (e.g. *tap*, *tree*, *treasure*, *tiger*, *toes*, *tent*, *teddy*, *tractor*, *turtle*, *tacos*, *trainers*)

Read 2: Prosody

- Read pages 6 and 7 using different tones.
  - Encourage the children to read page 6 in an instructional or teacherly voice.
  - Move on to the sounds of **tap tap** in the picture on page 7. Can they read the words and make them sound like the sticks hitting the pan?

Read 3: Comprehension

- Discuss any musical instruments the children can play, and what they have to do to play different notes.
- Read page 8. Ask: What is tipping? (*the pans at the top*)
- Talk about the steel pan, and whether they have heard one being played. Ask the children: What other instruments is it similar to? (*percussion instruments*, e.g. *drums*, *cymbals*)